MISSION COLLEGE
LEARNING RESOURCE SERVICE

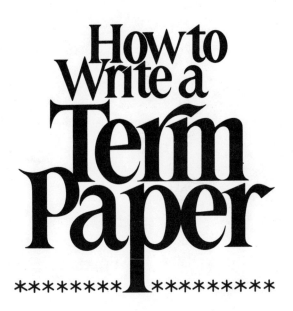

How to Write a Term Paper

********* *********

How to Write a Term Paper

****

Elizabeth James and Carol Barkin

With an Introduction by Leland B. Jacobs, Ph.D.

Lothrop, Lee & Shepard Books
New York

Printed in the United States of America.

6 7 8 9 10

Library of Congress Cataloging in Publication Data

James, Elizabeth.
   How to write a term paper.

   Bibliography: p.
   Includes index.
   Summary: Presents advice on how to select a topic, plan one's time, do research, organize notes, make an outline, and write an original term paper including footnotes.
   1. Report writing—Juvenile literature. 2. Research—Juvenile literature. [1. Report writing. 2. Research] I. Barkin, Carol, joint author. II. Title.
   LB1047.3.J35   808'.02   80-13734
   ISBN 0-688-45025-3 (pbk.)
   ISBN 0-688-51951-2 (lib. bdg.)

With thanks to Chaucy Bennetts,
our editor par excellence

Contents

Contents

To the Student

The first time I read *How to Write a Term Paper*, I kept thinking how sorry I was for all those students who never had this book when faced with doing an assignment in this kind of composition. But you are fortunate. You have these pages that not only give you essential information, but also present that information in such an appealing, readable style.

James and Barkin know those aspects of term-paper writing on which students seem always to need help. They describe for you the kinds of term papers you may be asked to write. They take careful note of the problems and give you practical suggestions for finding a topic to write about; for getting the topic in focus; for doing research and taking notes. As they write about such matters they zero in with specific recommendations. They don't settle for vague over-generalizations. Neither are they narrowly prescriptive or picayune.

James and Barkin will give you considerable

help on the writing of your term paper. From producing an outline and starting your rough draft to putting the paper in final form, the authors will deftly lead you through technical matters, offering practical suggestions for making your writing clear, well-ordered, and interesting. They don't tell you the writing will be easy or quickly accomplished. But they do propose that it can be quite a pleasant experience and that it is more creative than "conjugating verbs or memorizing theorems."

I think you will enjoy the way James and Barkin present their ideas. You'll quickly see that these writers aren't stuffy, pedantic, priggish. You'll see, too, that they're on your side, that they want to speak to you directly. And they give a great deal of pointed, practical help in only a few pages.

I confidently recommend James and Barkin as capable, lively guides for each step of the way in your term-paper writing, from starting point to that moment when your finished product is in hand.

Leland B. Jacobs, Ph.D.
Professor Emeritus of Education
Teachers College, Columbia University

I

What Makes a Good Term Paper?

Not many people sit down to write a term paper just for fun. Let's face it. Most term papers get written because they were assigned as a requirement for a class. Teachers assign term papers because they want to find out whether you can (1) do research on a specific topic and (2) put together what you have learned from your research in an orderly and clear presentation.

A really good term paper is also interesting. This may seem obvious, but too many term papers are clearly the result of a few rushed hours unwillingly spent at the last minute. If you are intrigued by your subject, your enthusiasm will come through in your writing. It never hurts to turn in a paper that's enjoyable to read. And if you've got something new to say, that's even better!

Just Give Me the Facts

One kind of term paper is basically an overview or summary of what you have learned about a specific subject. You might be writing about "Union Spies in the Civil War": this could be a factual account of how many there were, how and where they operated, and whom they reported to, leading up to a summation of the role they played in the war as a whole.

Or you might choose to write about "Simple Machines: What They Are and How They Work." The title here says it all. Your paper will be a straightforward description of the six simple machines (lever, wedge, inclined plane, pulley, wheel and axle, and screw), with an explanation of how they are used, and everyday examples for each one.

In both of these papers, you are not setting out to convert readers to your point of view. Your aim is to tell them the facts about a particular topic. In the "Spies" paper, you might conclude with an opinion, based on your research, about the effectiveness of the spy system, but the body of the paper will be an explanation of how it worked.

In the "Simple Machines" project, you're dealing with facts that are not subject to interpretation. Here your task is to explain these facts as clearly and interestingly as possible.

You might think of these as "objective" reports: your aim is to present the facts as objectively as you can.

What's Your Opinion?

At other times you may write term papers that express your opinion on the subject you're writing about. For example, a paper on "Was Lincoln an Effective Political Leader?" calls for your own conclusion, based on the facts you found through research. Or you might write on "The PLO: Is Terrorism Ever Justified?" Both of these topics require you to take sides on a question. You must research both sides of the issue before deciding which position is better supported by the facts.

This kind of term paper is a "point of view" report. Your purpose is to present evidence that shows why you favor your position.

Help Stamp Out Procrastination!

It's fatally easy to put off working on a long-term project like a term paper. You have so many things that are due the very next day, like your math homework and French assignment, and of course you have basketball practice or a baby-sitting job or your part in the class play to work on. Just remember that talking on the phone with your best friend about how much you don't want to do this term paper doesn't count as research!

If you find it hard to get started on a project with a due date several weeks off, try breaking it down into smaller pieces. Make your own assignments. The first week will be for doing the research; you'll have the outline done by the end of the second week; and the third week can then be reserved for writing the paper itself.

This is called "planning your time wisely." You've heard about it all the way through school and you've probably paid no attention to this kind of good advice. But think about it this way: you're going to have to write this term paper one way or the other. And you'll end up spending about the same amount of time either way you do it. If you wait until the last minute, you'll still have to do your library research, construct your outline, and get those ten pages written. But what you lose that way is the chance to let your brain mull things over while you're doing other things.

Why should you care? What good will it do to mull things over? Take a tip from people who write for a living: the "back of your brain" is the best source of inspiration. Contrary to what you might expect, sitting down to write your paper the minute you finish your research generally results in a hodgepodge of other people's ideas without any unifying thread.

If you get your research done early, you can take a day or two off and "forget" about it. While you're painting scenery for the play and reading the new assignment for English, all those facts will be percolating away on their own. Then, when you do sit down to think out your term paper, you'll be amazed at how they've fallen into place. A little distance helps you see connections and conclusions that probably wouldn't have occurred to you when you'd just finished your research.

Even if you don't quite believe this, why not give it a try? The worst that will happen is that you'll turn your term paper in on time—always a point in your favor! And you may find it a pleasant change to produce a well-thought-out piece of work instead of the fuzzy ramblings of an all-night marathon.

2

Where to Begin?

The first thing to do is to find out exactly what is expected of you in writing your term paper. This may sound a little simpleminded, but you'd be surprised at the number of people who sit down to start writing and suddenly discover they don't know what goes where.

Write It Down!

When the assignment is given, be sure to write everything down. Ask questions if there's anything you're not sure about. Here are the things you should know:

- What kinds of topics are acceptable? Is there a list of topics to choose from, or can you come up with your own topic? *yes*
- How long should the paper be? This will affect the kind of topic you choose. *3 4*
- What will you have to turn in? Besides the

finished paper, does your teacher want to see your outline or your first draft? *\graph*

- Is there a specific form your paper should follow? For example, do you need a title page? Where should your name, the name of the class, and the page number go on each page? How big should the margins be? Would your teacher prefer a binder, stapled pages, or just a paper clip to hold your paper together?
- Are there requirements about the research sources you use? Do you need a bibliography of at least five sources? Are you supposed to have a certain number of footnotes?
- What form should the footnotes follow? How about the bibliography? Should the footnotes go at the bottom of each page or should they be grouped in a list at the end of the paper?
- Will you be penalized for errors in spelling and punctuation? If your teacher is one who gives an automatic "F" for a single spelling mistake, this is something you should know about in advance!
- When is the paper due?

Your teacher may hand out a mimeographed sheet with this information all collected in one place. If you have other questions, don't rely on your memory: jot down the answers to them on this same sheet. And then, try not to lose it!

Find a Topic That Turns You On

The key to a terrific term paper is to write about a topic that you think is really interesting. If there's a list of subjects to choose from, pick the one you'd enjoy learning more about. But what if you've been assigned a topic, and it's one you couldn't care less about? With a little thought, you can surely come up with an aspect of it that intrigues you. Take the topic "Everyday Life During the Revolutionary War." Boring? Not at all! How about using your interest in clothes, and researching the way the colonists dressed and the problems they faced when they couldn't get fabric from England? Or if you like watching the stock market, perhaps you could investigate what happened to the money supply and how this affected people's ability to buy and sell. Of course, it's wise to check with your teacher before getting heavily involved, but there's always something about a topic that you can work up some enthusiasm for.

But suppose the sky is the limit: you can choose your own topic from any area you've covered so far in class. It's great to be able to pick out something that grabs you. Just keep in mind that the scope of your subject should correspond to the length your term paper is supposed to be. It's easy to get carried away. You won't be able to do justice to the entire Civil War in ten pages. Even if you choose something like "Popular Music of the Civil War Era," you may find there's far too much material to cover. Consider narrowing the topic further, perhaps to include only "Army Songs of the Civil War." Then you'll really be able to say something about the songs—your ten pages won't be filled up with a list of titles.

On the other hand, you may find that your topic is too narrow to begin with. Or your library may not have enough material and you'll be unable to research an obscure subject. "Cattle Brands of the Old West" sounds like a big subject, but you may not be able to find much information about it. Perhaps you could broaden the topic to something like "Cattle Rustling on the Open Range"; then branding would be one section of the paper.

Ask your teacher's advice about the topic you've chosen: is it too big or too small, and is it appropriate for the course? Teachers love to be consulted. It makes them feel someone is paying attention in class!

Since you'll be putting in a lot of effort on your term paper, you'll want to think of a subject that will be worth all that time and trouble. Even if it's not your favorite class, there's bound to be something about what you're studying that strikes a spark.

You may even come up with a really creative way of approaching the problem. Instead of a straightforward account of how the Underground Railway worked, have you thought of inventing a series of letters or a diary written by a person in charge of one of the secret way-stations for runaway slaves? This might be an exciting way to present your research on how many slaves passed through and the kinds of problems they faced. You could include footnoted facts and quotations from speeches and news articles of the time.

If your creative bent runs to plays or poetry, think up a way to use this talent in a term paper. Writing a dramatic version of the moving scene in which Lee surrendered to Grant at Appomattox could be a way to make the facts you've learned come alive to the reader.

Once Over Lightly at the Library

When you've decided on a topic you'd like to write about, make a preliminary visit to the library.

Your purpose is to find out what resources are available for research on that specific subject. Take a look at the encyclopedias; check the big dictionary (you may be surprised at the tidbits and leads you'll pick up); and make a quick run through the card catalogue. If you can't find a single thing that pertains to your topic, you'd better change your plan. But if there seems to be plenty of good stuff to look up, you're on your way!

3

What Do You
Need to Know?

Now that you've got a preliminary topic in mind for your term paper, take a few moments to think about it. What do you want to know about this subject? What questions will your term paper attempt to answer?

Suppose you have chosen to write about China's "Gang of Four," the political leaders of the early 1970s. Here are some questions you might set out to answer:

Who were the Gang of Four?
What did they do?
When were they in power?
What happened to them?

Of course, as you read you may find other aspects of your topic that you want to pursue. But starting out with a list of questions to be answered is a good way to focus your research and keep it from going off in all directions.

Look It Up!

By this time you undoubtedly know where the library is, and how to use its resources. After all, teachers have been telling you about it since you were in the first grade. But doing serious research is not the same thing as browsing for a good novel to read; if you find you need some help, don't hesitate to ask the librarian.

Encyclopedias

You've already checked the encyclopedia, but now is the time to take another look. Many articles have cross-references at the end, referring the reader to other articles on related subjects. Not only is it helpful to glance through these other articles for useful information, but the references are good clues for topics to look under in the card catalogue.

Some encyclopedias also provide short "bibliographies" at the ends of some articles. Again, this is a helpful starting point in your search for books on the subject.

There are specialized encyclopedias that are arranged in different ways. The Encyclopedia of

American History, for example, gives a chronological account of events like the Civil War; it's especially helpful if you want to know what was going on in various parts of the country at a particular time. Other reference books may have another slant on a subject. There are works devoted to science, famous people, geography, or literature. All these books are in the reference section of your library, and the reference librarian not only can show you where they are but can tell you about some you haven't even heard of.

Books

The card catalogue will be your main research tool. As you know, it is a complete alphabetical list of every book in the library, filed under both the book's title and the author's name. Cards are usually filed under a subject heading as well. For example, if your topic is Lee's surrender at Appomattox, here are some likely subject headings to check: Lee, Robert E.; Grant, Ulysses S.; Appomattox. Then try the large subject heading "U.S.—History"; this is subdivided chronologically, so you'll probably find something under "Civil War."

There may be a whole slew of books under these various subject headings. How do you decide which ones will be useful? The card itself contains several clues. First, what is the book's title? If it's *Robert E. Lee: The Early Years* or *General Grant and the Indian Wars,* don't bother with it. Because of the time frame, it won't have anything about Appomattox.

Check the length of the book; the card tells you the number of pages it has. A brief history of the whole Civil War in 124 pages is unlikely to have much detail on a single event like Appomattox. On the other hand, if it's a three-volume tome on the war, you'll only need volume three.

Catalogue cards also provide a brief description of what the book contains, which may help you decide whether it's worth looking at. Toward the bottom of the card is a list of the other places the book is listed in the catalogue; this can often give you a new idea about subject headings to check on.

When you find a card for a book that looks promising, get out your pencil and paper. This is the moment to write down all the information you could possibly need on this book. Nothing is more annoying than to have to look things up

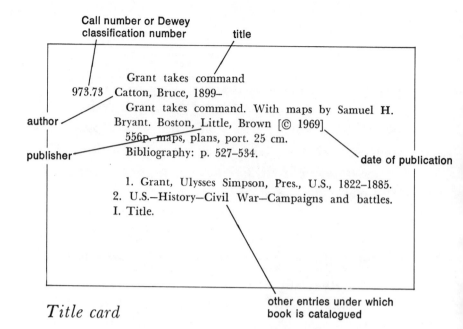

Call number or Dewey classification number

title

973.73   Catton, Bruce, 1899–

      Grant takes command

author

      Grant takes command. With maps by Samuel H. Bryant. Boston, Little, Brown [© 1969]

publisher   556p. maps, plans, port. 25 cm.
      Bibliography: p. 527–534.

date of publication

    1. Grant, Ulysses Simpson, Pres., U.S., 1822–1885.
    2. U.S.–History–Civil War–Campaigns and battles.
    I. Title.

Title card

other entries under which book is catalogued

GRANT, ULYSSES SIMPSON, PRESIDENT U.S., 1822–1885.

973.73   Catton, Bruce, 1899–
      Grant takes command. With maps by Samuel H. Bryant. Boston, Little, Brown [© 1969]
      556p. maps, plans, port. 25 cm.
      Bibliography: p. 527–534.

    1. Grant, Ulysses Simpson, Pres., U.S. 1822–1885.
    2. U.S.–History–Civil War–Campaigns and battles.
    I. Title.

Subject card

U.S.–HISTORY–CIVIL WAR–
CAMPAIGNS AND BATTLES

973.73 Catton, Bruce, 1899–
     Grant takes command. With maps by Samuel H.
Bryant. Boston, Little, Brown [© 1969]
     556p. maps, plans, port. 25 cm.
     Bibliography: p. 527–534.

     1. Grant, Ulysses Simpson, Pres., U.S., 1822–1885.
2. U.S.–History–Civil War–Campaigns and battles.
I. Title.

Subject card

973.73 Catton, Bruce, 1899–
     Grant takes command. With maps by Samuel H.
Bryant. Boston, Little, Brown [© 1969]
     556p. maps, plans, port. 25 cm.
     Bibliography: p. 527–534.

     1. Grant, Ulysses Simpson, Pres., U.S., 1822–1885.
2. U.S.–History–Civil War–Campaigns and battles.
I. Title.

Author card

two or three times because you forgot to note down the book's call number or the author's name. You need the book's call number; the author's name; the full title of the book; the publisher's name and the date and place of publication.

Why should you bother with all this detail? First, of course, you'll need the call number in order to find the book on the shelves. Then, if the book is out, you'll need call number, author, and title to fill out a request slip to hand to the librarian. If the book turns out to be useful, you'll eventually list it in your bibliography, and all the other information will be needed then. So you might as well write it all down now and save yourself some trouble.

Magazines and Journals

Especially valuable in writing a term paper on current or recent events are articles in magazines. The way to locate articles on your subject is to consult the *Readers' Guide to Periodical Literature*. This is a series of large volumes found in the library's reference section; each volume is an index of articles published in over one hundred

magazines during a period of a year or more. Supplementary paperbound volumes list articles published during the current year.

If your paper is on China's "Gang of Four," the *Readers' Guide* is for you. Why? Because this is recent history, and there may be few if any books in the library that mention it. What you need is articles in magazines like *Time, Newsweek,* and *U.S. News & World Report.*

Since the *Readers' Guide* is organized chronologically, get the volume for the years in which the Gang of Four was in the news. Look under the subject heading "China" and find the subheadings that are relevant. Be sure to look at the *"See also"* at the end of each listing for other likely subject headings. And of course you can look under more specific headings like "Gang of Four" and the names of the individuals for possible articles.

Here again, consider each article's potential usefulness before you fill out a request slip for every single one. An article listed as "The Gang of Four: Effect on International Finance" may not be very helpful if you're only concerned with their activities inside China.

The front of each volume explains how the *Guide* works and lists the abbreviations used. Most libraries mark this list to show which magazines they subscribe to. There's no use asking for an article from a particular magazine if the library doesn't have copies of it.

When you come across an article that sounds good, write down all the pertinent information: author's name, title of the article, name of the magazine it appeared in, date of that issue of the magazine, and page numbers of the article. You'll need all this both to ask for the magazine from the periodical loan desk and to list the article in your bibliography.

Your school library may not have a *Readers' Guide*, so you may be doing this research at the public library. Before you trek down there, consider your topic. If it's Appomattox, you're not likely to find many magazine articles you can use!

Other Resources

Where else can you look for resource material? For current events, you may want to search out newspaper articles. Your local newspaper undoubtedly has a file of back issues. And large libraries have indexes of articles in *The New York Times* and the *Wall Street Journal*. You can look at them on microfilm.

If the topic of your paper falls into the province of a governmental department or agency, you can write to ask for pamphlets on that subject. Try both state and federal agencies, and explain the project you're working on. If you think this might be a fruitful method, write your letter early and tell them when you need the information; government agencies are not always as speedy as you might hope.

Be inventive! After all, the more resources you consult, the better grasp you'll have of all sides of the issue. For a paper on capital punishment, why not write to a prison warden, a judge, even a prisoner, to ask what they think? Tracking down unusual sources of information can be fun, and your detective work will unearth lots of material from which to draw a well-informed conclusion of your own.

How about resources closer to home? Local museums often have leaflets and other informative material on various subjects. Or, if your term paper is about an event in your town's history, you may be able to find people who were there when it happened. Personal interviews can give you a fresh slant and they will make your reader feel as though he were there. Veterans of World War II, Korea, or Vietnam may be cooperative and willing to talk to you about their experiences. Of course, you'll be careful to take accurate notes, and if you quote someone, it's wise to check with him or her to make sure you've got it right.

Make a Note of It

The notes you make as you do your research are the foundation of the term paper you will eventually write. You can think of them as the bricks without which you can't build a solidly constructed report. Your notes are in fact the result of the time you spend in research, which may well be the largest bloc of time you spend in preparing the paper.

So don't think of them as mere hasty scribbles you can jot on any handy scrap of paper. If your notes aren't legible and understandable to you, you might as well not have bothered to make them—you'll just have to go back and plow through the books you've already read.

It doesn't much matter what system of note-taking you use, so long as it works for you. Some people find they like the traditional method of using file cards; each card should contain a single quote, fact, or group of facts, along with the name of the reference source and the page number. Often a heading is used at the top of the card to indicate the general topic each note applies to.

Using file cards makes it easy to move bits of information around as you work on the structure of your outline. However, you may find it both cumbersome and distracting to write down your notes this way as you are reading. You might

---

Effectiveness of Confederate spy system

" . . . a Confederate army was never surprised in an important engagement of the war."

Miller, Photog. Hist. ~~article~~ section by Charles King, p. 288.

prefer to use regular notebook paper and make a list of notes as they occur in each source you read. If you do it this way, be sure to write the name of the source at the beginning of the list, and include the source page number next to each note you take. It's helpful to leave a line or two of space between the notes; then you can easily tell where one ends and the next begins. Whether you use file cards or notebook paper, write on one side of the paper only. It's easy to forget to look at the backs of your note pages. Besides, later on you'll want to be able to spread out all your notes at once and see everything you've got.

A third method of note-taking combines elements of both these systems. Think about the main questions you intend to answer in your term paper; write each of these at the top of a separate sheet of notebook paper. What if you are writing about "Confederate Spies in the Civil War"? Here is how your notes on your first two sources might look:

LIST OF SOURCES

Miller, Francis Trevelyan, ed. *The Photographic History of the Civil War in Ten Volumes.* Vol. 8, New York: The Review of Reviews Co., 1912.

Bakeless, John. *Spies of the Confederacy.* Philadelphia: J. B. Lippincott Co., 1970.

Question 1: Who were the Confederate spies?

MILLER (section on Confed. spies written by Capt. John W. Headley)

p. 288: many names not known because they worked in secrecy

p. 289: Mrs. Greenhow, ran spy ring in Washington

p. 290: many were officers—e.g., Col. J. Stoddard Johnson, in charge of spies on Gen. Bragg's staff, & Headley (author of article)

p. 291: female spies—Belle Boyd, Southern belle who was famous Confed. spy

p. 292: civilians—e.g., Henry B. Shaw (a.k.a. Dr. C. E. Coleman, Capt. C. E. Coleman), former steamboat clerk, had knowledge of middle Tennessee; in charge of famous band of spies

p. 295: many Confed. spies were cavalrymen used for this purpose (Vespasian Chancellor worked for J. E. B. Stuart)

p. 299: other civilians—Lytle, photographer from Baton Rouge, member of Confed. secret service, got valuable info in photos and sent to Confed. command

BAKELESS

p. 2: many Confed. spies were Southerners living in Washington since before war; many had been in gov't. or still were

p. 15: many volunteer spies—"complete amateurs"—gave helpful info

p. 30: civilian spies—3 doctors (worked for J. E. B. Stuart)

p. 65: ". . . a number of Southern women residing in the North continued to spy right through the war."

Question 2: How were they organized?

MILLER (by Headley)

p. 286: "The Confederate States had no such secret-service organization as was developed and used by the Federal Government during the Civil War, and yet it is probably true that, in the matter of obtaining needed military information, the Confederacy was, on the whole, better served than was the North."

p. 288: Confed. State Dept. had reg. courier service between Richmond and Maryland; agents used newspapers to communicate

p. 290: every general had own spies and cavalry scouts

BAKELESS

pp. 2–3: Confeds. had secret service before war; helped by big secret society (Knights of Golden Circle)

p. 6: 3 diff. Confed. spy rings in Washington during war (run by Mrs. Greenhow, Capt. Conrad, Frank Stringfellow)

p. 6: Confed. Signal Service est. 1862—really spy service (1st one centralized for Confeds.)

Question 3: How effective were they and why?

MILLER (by Chas. King)

p. 18: South had much better info than North —unity of belief in cause

p. 22: as North moved down, folk behind lines were for South, also Confeds. lived in Washington

p. 288: ". . . a Confederate army was never surprised in an important engagement of the war."

BAKELESS

p. 2: effective because est. before begin. of war

p. 4: lax Union security made access to info easy

p. 5: people willing to serve; widespread fanatical loyalty to South

Notice that on the note sheets only the author's last name is used to identify the source. Keep a complete list of your sources as you use them on a separate sheet, with all the bibliographical information included for each one. Of course, as you do your research, other headings to group notes under will occur to you. Just add another page to your set of notes for each new concept.

Whatever system you use, there are a few things to keep in mind:

- Include the page number as part of every note you take.
- Copy down quotations exactly.
- Note specific facts clearly and fully.

All of these will help keep your note-taking to a one-step operation, and you won't have to go back and recheck what you've already written.

Notes are supposed to summarize the material you've read and help you remember the main ideas and important points. Be brief—if you need as many words for your notes as the author needed in the first place, you'll be spending far too much time writing them and they'll be too long to plow through later on. At the same time, don't make your notes so sketchy that you can't understand them when you go back over them; a note that reads "Org. gd., clever—mid-1863" won't help you recall much of the author's description of the superb way the spy system was working in the middle of the Civil War.

Use your own words to summarize the ideas and facts you want to note down. Why is this important? For three reasons.

First, restating a passage in your own words ensures that you really understand what the author has said. Then when you reread your notes you'll get the point right away, without having to stop and figure out what they're supposed to mean.

Second, summarizing in new phrases, instead of condensing the author's words, keeps you from unconsciously plagiarizing someone else's work. If you've paraphrased the author's original sentences, you may not remember when you sit down to write whether your notes are your wording or the author's. Well-put phrases from your notes will certainly appear in your final paper, so just make sure they're your own!

Finally, using scraps of sentences from a number of different authors will give your final paper a very uneven style. Putting things in your own words from the beginning will help carry your individual tone through the whole paper and give it a style of its own.

A last word: unless you have to turn them in, there's no need for your notes to be super-neat. They're just for your own use, so the only thing that matters is that you can understand what they mean!

4

What Are You Trying to Say?

Now you've finished your research. You've closed the last book and taken the last note. Of course, there is always another book or two you could have looked into, and probably there are a few more notes you could have taken.

But call a halt. You've located the useful sources on your topic and gone through them. Even if you have time to spare now, there's no point in digging through the less relevant works in search of that one elusive reference—it will turn out to be something you read in all your major sources anyway. Nobody expects you to turn in a Ph.D. thesis; the length of your paper doesn't allow for an unlimited amount of detail.

Besides, your time can be better spent now. Assuming you started doing your research early in the game, you have the advantage of being able to put your notes away for a day or two. Relax; put your mind on "automatic pilot"; think about something entirely different. All that information will bubble away quietly without any effort on your part, and that mishmash of facts and quotes and ideas will start coming together.

Don't worry that you'll forget everything you've read. You won't. And you've always got your notes to remind you. What you may forget is the elegant phrasing of one or two authors, and that's all to the good; when you start writing, you won't slip into someone else's words.

After a short "vacation" you'll come back to your project with renewed enthusiasm. You may even see it from a fresh point of view, finding an approach you didn't know was there.

Take a Look at What You've Got

When you get out your notes again, read through them. Try to pretend this is the first time you've seen this information. What have you got to work with? Is there a lot of detail on one especially fascinating aspect of your topic? Maybe that should be the major theme of your term paper.

On the other hand, perhaps your sources didn't have much to say about the topic you originally planned to write on. Or maybe your original idea now seems pretty dull and another twist on the same facts looks more exciting. That's fine.

There's no law that says you can't shift the emphasis or revise your original concept. If you're really interested in what you're writing about, your paper will be a lot more lively. Let's say the topic you researched was "How Colonial Houses Were Built." You might have found some information on house-building, but you thought it was kind of boring and repetitious. As you reread your notes, you realize that the early colonists faced a harsher climate than they were used to, and they had to adapt their house designs to withstand the colder winters. You have notes on where fireplaces were put and what kinds of insulation and windows were used. So, why not change your topic to "Colonial Houses: Designed for a New Climate"?

The idea is to use the information you found and took down in your notes. Don't feel you have to stretch a few skimpy tidbits on your original topic; instead, use the wealth of good stuff you unearthed on a different aspect of the topic to construct a full and well-rounded paper.

Come Up with a One-Liner

Now that you know exactly what your topic is, are you ready to sit down and write? Not quite.

First you need to state the main idea of your paper in one or at the most two sentences.

This "summary sentence" is not the same as the topic you've chosen or the title of your paper. It is a brief description of what your reader will learn about the topic after reading your paper. For the paper on Confederate spies, your title might be "Spies in Gray." Your summary sentence could be "The excellence of the Confederate spy system, both military and civilian, arose out of devotion to the South's cause, early organization, and easy access to enemy information." This may not be the most elegant sentence you've ever written, but it expresses what you want to tell your reader about this subject.

If you can't write a summary sentence for your paper, you haven't thought things through well enough yet; you don't have a clear idea of what you want your paper to say. Don't skip this important step; take time to figure out where you're going. Otherwise your paper will end up sounding disorganized and unfocused. Your readers won't get the point, because you won't know what point you're trying to make.

Your summary sentence will be a useful reference point as you go through the remaining stages in writing your paper. It helps you organize your outline in a logical progression of thought. You'll refer back to it as you write, to make sure you're not straying too far afield. And, best of all, it gives you a sense of confidence from the outset—you feel as if you know what you're doing!

5

Why Make an Outline?

You may have asked yourself this question many times. Why do you have to bother with the extra work of making an outline before you write your paper? Is it just another cruel form of torture that teachers have dreamed up to make students' lives miserable?

Of course the answer is "no." (What did you expect in a book your teacher recommended?) And in spite of what you've been told, it's not just because it's good practice for all the writing you're going to do later on. You may have decided you never want to write anything longer than a postcard!

The real reason for making an outline is that it makes writing your paper a whole lot easier. Sounds peculiar, but it's true. Most experienced writers wouldn't dream of starting a book without a good outline to work from. Some people even make outlines for the letters they write.

Your outline is the basis of the organization of your paper. You might think of it as a map you will follow when you sit down to write the finished product. The outline shows the way you will develop each idea and how you will move from one idea to the next. And the more complete your outline is, the more useful it will be to you.

An outline does two things. It lists the major points you plan to cover and the order in which you will present them. Also, it gathers the subpoints you want to include under each major point.

Look back at your summary sentence. It will probably give you some clues about what your major points are and how they can be arranged in a logical order. The summary sentence for the paper on Confederate spies was: "The excellence of the Confederate spy system, both military and civilian, arose out of devotion to the South's cause, early organization, and easy access to enemy information."

What clues does this give you? First you'll have to show that the Confederates had an excellent spy system and describe both the military and civilian segments. This is your first major point. Then you will want to give examples and explanations for the three contributing factors in turn.

Your outline would then look like this:

I. Excellence of Confederate spy system
   —acclaimed by all
   —better than Union spy system
II. Military spy system
   —each general had own spies: examples
   —important role of cavalry: examples
III. Civilian spy system
   —in Washington: examples
   —behind advancing Union lines: examples
   —many different professions and walks of life:
     examples
IV. Fanatical loyalty to South
   —made people want to be spies
   —made them willing to work without pay
   —made them risk their lives
V. Early organization
   —many Southerners already in Washington
   —South active before actual war
VI. Easy access to Union information
   —Washington gossip
   —lax Union security
   —Southern sympathizers in Union govern-
     ment bureaucracy
   —Union secret service overtaxed with prob-
     lems

Now you have a preliminary outline. Take a look at it. Does it make sense? Could it be better organized?

This outline could be organized a lot better. First of all, it doesn't seem to have much of a conclusion or wrap-up. Also, the points really fall into two main categories: how the system was organized, and why it worked so well. That leaves you with some information about the excellence of the system as an introduction. You can end the paper with your conclusion: that the reason those people were so willing and did such a good job was that they were really devoted to their cause.

Your revised outline would then look like this:

I. Excellence of Confederate spy system
   —acclaimed by all
   —better than Union spy system
II. How it worked
   —military spy system
   • each general had own spies: examples
   • important role of cavalry: examples
   —civilian spy system
   • in Washington: examples
   • behind advancing Union lines: examples

　　• many different professions and walks of
　　　life: examples

III. Why it worked so well
　　—early organization
　　　• many Southerners already in Washington
　　　• South active before actual war
　　—easy access to Union information
　　　• Washington gossip
　　　• lax Union security
　　　• Southern sympathizers in Union govern-
　　　　ment bureaucracy
　　　• Union secret service overtaxed with prob-
　　　　lems.

IV. Fanatical loyalty to South as common factor
　　—made people want to be spies
　　—made them willing to work without pay
　　—made them risk their lives

Of course, this is not a complete outline. It
doesn't show all the subheadings you will deal
with under each major heading, although it gives
a few possibilities. And it is phrased inconsistently.
But it does give you a rough picture of how your
paper will be constructed.

There are lots of ways to organize your material. If your subject is biographical or a description of a particular event, you may want to begin

at the beginning and go on until the end, in chronological order. If you're taking sides on a question, it might be best to present the arguments for your position, followed by the arguments against it, and then wrap up with an explanation of why your position is the stronger one. And if your paper is an explanation of how a government body or economic system works, you could begin with the simple elements and work up to the more complex ones.

The idea is to use your head about this. Pretend you're explaining the subject of your paper to someone who knows nothing about it. What would he or she need to know first? What's the logical way to proceed from there? Think about how you arrived at the conclusion stated in your summary sentence; then write down the step-by-step chain of reasoning that got you there. This can be the basis of your outline.

Is It Formal or Informal?

Some teachers are sticklers for the "correct" form for an outline. If your teacher feels this way and if you have to turn in your outline, you'd probably better do it according to the standard method.

This actually isn't very hard. Here is a sample of a formal outline:

I. First Course
   A. Cranberry salad mold
   B. Relish tray
      1. carrot sticks
      2. celery sticks
      3. olives
         a. green
         b. black
   C. Rolls and butter
II. Main Course
   A. Turkey
      1. stuffing
      2. gravy
      3. cranberry sauce
   B. Baked yams
   C. Green beans
      1. butter
      2. lemon wedges
III. Dessert
   A. Pumpkin pie or mince pie
      1. whipped cream
      2. hard sauce

B. Coffee or tea
   1. milk or cream
   2. sugar
   3. lemon wedges

You may be tempted to add "IV. Delicious!" as a conclusion. And you've probably figured out that this outline could be entitled "Thanksgiving Dinner." But did your eagle eye notice that this outline is chronological? It starts when people sit down to the table and moves through time until they push their chairs back with a sigh of pleasure!

Looking at a dinner menu in outline form makes it easy to see how a formal outline works. The Roman numerals indicate the major sections that compose the whole. Under each Roman numeral heading, each capital letter subheading has equal importance. Each Arabic number under a capital letter indicates a division of that sub-head. And so on. Thus, the writer of this outline did not list olives as "3. green olives

4. black olives."

Instead, the category of "olives" was subdivided into "green" and "black." (Following this outline to its logical conclusion, you would expect the relish tray to be divided into three equal sections

—for carrots, celery, and olives—and the olive section to contain as many green olives as black.)

You may have noticed that in this outline, every time a category is subdivided there are at least two entries in that subdivision. This is because if you divide something, you have to end up with at least two smaller parts. If you have only one entry in a subdivision, it's not really a subdivision—it's part of the preceding larger heading. In the menu outline, item I. C. is "Rolls and butter," even though item II. C. "Green beans" has "butter" as a subdivision, along with "lemon wedges." If there had been a choice of margarine or butter for the rolls, these would have been subdivisions 1. and 2. under I. C.

Another requirement of a formal outline is that there must be grammatical consistency in every division. That means that all Roman numeral headings must be either phrases or sentences, not a mixture of both, and all other subheads on the same level must be phrased the same way. In the menu outline, if heading I. had been "What's the first course?", headings II. and III. would have also been questions—"What's the main course?" and "What's for dessert?" The rest of the outline could have remained the same. But if one capital letter heading had been phrased as an imperative sentence—"Enjoy a smooth cranberry salad mold"—the other capital letter headings would also have had to be phrased the same way—"Sample the crisp relish tray" or "Bite into hot rolls and butter."

A good outline is like a menu—it tells you what's coming up next. For any kind of subject, an outline could also be a Table of Contents. When you outline your paper, be sure your reader won't be confused by finding dessert instead of the main course.

This standard form for outlines works well for many people, and it's particularly helpful when your topic is a complicated one. However, an outline is a working tool for a writer, and you have to put yours together in a way that works well for you. If you're more comfortable with underlines, dashes, and indentations to show the subdivisions of your topic, that's fine. If you prefer headings that are phrased as questions, that's okay too. Just make sure you know what everything means, so your outline will be a help and not a puzzle.

Whatever form your outline takes, it should show you where new sections of your paper begin. Within each section, an outline should serve as a guide for beginning new paragraphs and should indicate what each paragraph will cover. This won't always work out exactly—you may need two or three paragraphs for some subsections—but the outline should signal each new step in your train of thought and help you follow your way to the conclusion.

Shuffle the Deck and Deal Them Out!

Once you have your outline fairly well organized, you need to match up your notes and quotes with the various sections and subsections of the outline. This is the point where the wisdom of putting only one note or quote on each index card, or leaving spaces between them if they are on sheets of paper, strikes home! If you have taken the time to write clear, legible notes in the first place, you will have a much easier time gathering the material you need for each section of the paper.

The first step is to number the divisions of your outline if you haven't done so already. This numbering system doesn't have to be very elaborate, especially for an informal outline, but you need some sort of shorthand label for each section.

Now go through your notes and decide which

section each one belongs in. Label each note with the correct section number. If you've put your notes on index cards, you can simply arrange them in order. But be sure to number them anyway—if you drop the stack of cards, you'll have to start all over! If you have used sheets of paper for your notes, then write the section numbers in the margin beside each note. It's a good idea to use a colored pen or pencil for this numbering so you can spot the numbers at a glance.

Of course, under each section number, you'll have to decide what you want to say first. You can always use another set of numbers or letters within each section. But if it starts getting too confusing to flip back and forth through your pages of notes, why not simply cut them up? Since you have written on only one side of the paper and have left space between the notes, it will be easy to transform your note sheets into "file cards."

Once you've identified the notes that fit into each section of your outline, it may turn out that you have a few notes left over. These are often odd bits of information that you thought might be useful. Don't feel you have to use them just because they're there.

Glance through your arrangement of notes and quotes and recheck your outline to make sure you've covered all the points. If your quotes are spread fairly evenly throughout your outline, you're in good shape. But if they are all clumped together in one or two places and your teacher has required at least one footnote on each page of your paper, you'll have to do a little adjusting. You might find that a few of the quotes will go just as well in another section. Or perhaps you can throw in some "footnote-able" facts where you don't have any quotes. However you work it, get this problem straightened out before you start writing—you'll have enough to think about then without also scrambling around for some tidbit to footnote!

Now that your desk is littered with little heaps of paper, sharpen your pencils. You're ready to write!

6

How Do You Put It into Words?

This is it! No matter how well you've done your research or how cleverly you've arranged your outline, you always end up at the point where you have to put pen to paper. The term paper itself is the end product of your research and your thinking. It's a little like baking a cake. When you're finished you don't have a couple of eggs and some flour and butter. These ingredients have been combined to create a whole new product. In the same way, when you've written your paper, you won't end up with a bunch of disconnected thoughts and some notes and quotes. These ingredients will have been combined to produce an interesting and coherent presentation.

Roughing It

Your first or "rough" draft isn't supposed to be a model of neatness. On the other hand, you do want to be able to read it. Use one side of the paper only. Write on every other line, leaving plenty of room for corrections or additions. Be sure to make a parenthetical note of the book and page number after each quotation or fact you plan to footnote—you don't want to have to shuffle through all those notes again to see where it came from! Use whatever cheap paper you like; everyone has to rewrite at least once.

Get Started!

Are you sitting at your desk tapping your teeth with your pencil, wondering what your first sentence should be? Getting started is always the hardest part. Don't wait for that perfect opening phrase—you may sit there all night! Plunge right in.

You might begin with your summary sentence or some variation of it. This tells the reader right away what your paper is about and is always a workable beginning. Or were you planning to use that summary sentence as the conclusion to your paper? You still can! Of course, you will reword it. And by the time you've reached the end of your paper, another wrap-up sentence may have struck you. This type of paper has the general format of telling the reader what you are going to say, saying it, and then telling the reader what you've said. This is a typical structure for scientific papers as well as for works on other subjects.

Another way to start is to use an interesting fact or offbeat anecdote as your opening. This can be in the form of a question or simply a statement. The idea is to pique your reader's curiosity and make him or her want to read on. Or how about beginning with a quotation or definition?

No matter how you begin, the important thing is to get started. You can always rewrite the opening once you are loosened up and writing along.

Watch Where You're Going!

Of course, after all the hard work you put into it you're going to keep a sharp eye on your outline. This may sound obvious, but sometimes people forget to make use of the outline they've prepared. Keep referring back to your outline and check off the notes as you use them. This will help you keep track of where you are going, so that you can move smoothly from one train of thought into the next. If you know what the next paragraph or section is going to be about, you'll be able to lead into it at the end of the part you're working on.

Make It Easy on Yourself

Do you think of writing as hard work? You're not alone. Many people have difficulty putting their thoughts on paper. But don't let yourself get psyched into thinking you can't do it. There are some ways of approaching a writing project that make it easier.

Don't worry about style at this point. You can get all hung up trying to think of fancy phrases and elegant words, and meanwhile you'll lose track of what you're saying. Just concentrate on getting it written down in the order you've planned.

You might pretend you're explaining your topic to a friend who is interested but not very knowledgeable. Try saying each sentence out loud; if it sounds good, write it down the way you said it. Your purpose is to present your information clearly and simply, so that your reader (or your friend) can follow your train of thought and understand it the first time through.

Another trick is to pretend you're explaining your ideas to your sweet elderly aunt. She wants to know what you have to say but she's not up-to-date on slang. If you write that President Lincoln was "heavy into reading," your aunt will be a little confused.

The idea is to steer a middle course between overly formal or fancy language on the one hand and slangy expressions on the other. Clear, simple sentences will get your message across to anyone who reads your paper.

Keep yourself from being overwhelmed by the length of the paper you have to write. It is much easier to think about writing a paragraph than a whole paper. So break up your outline into small sections and then deal with one section at a time. Say to yourself, "In this paragraph I want to explain X." Write that much and then worry about explaining Y in the next paragraph.

As you work on each section, write as much as you have to in order to get your point across. Don't worry about your paper's being too long. It's always easier to cut it down to the right length later on than to try to pad a paper that turns out too short.

Lack of information is usually not the reason

a paper is too short. You probably have plenty to say on your topic. But in your hurry to get the thing written, you may have skimped on explanations or left out examples that would support your points. You may think that if you can just get it done, you'll be able to go back and fill in the empty spaces afterward. But this method results in a patchy style; to make the new material work in smoothly, you have to rewrite the surrounding sections. It's easier and quicker in the long run to write everything down the first time through.

Give Credit Where It's Due

Everybody hates footnotes, right? They're tedious and boring. So why should you bother with them? There are two good reasons.

First, the author whose book you used as source material for your paper deserves to get some credit. After all, he or she did a lot of work in writing the book, and you found it useful in doing your research. Second, footnotes allow whoever reads your paper to check out what you have to say or to follow up on an aspect of your topic that may be covered more fully elsewhere. You might think of this as an extra service you're providing for your reader.

How do you know what to footnote? Of course, you always footnote direct quotes. But what about facts you cite to support your points? After all, everything in your paper—in fact, everything you know—is something you learned from a source. Obviously, you don't footnote every sentence.

Facts and Opinions

A good general rule to start from is that you need not footnote anything that is generally known. Such statements as "A President of the United States cannot serve more than two terms in office" or "Lincoln was shot by John Wilkes Booth in 1865" or "The first ten amendments to the U.S. Constitution are known as the Bill of Rights" can certainly be considered common knowledge and they should not be footnoted.

However, a fact that is little known—for example, "In 1790, the first census of the American population recorded 3,929,214 inhabitants"—needs a footnote to tell readers where you found this information. This category includes dates, numbers, scientific data, and so on. You must also footnote statements of fact that conflict with the opinion of most other authorities: if you say that King George III was secretly in sympathy with the American Revolution, you'd better be able to cite the source of this information! Finally, any statement of another writer's opinion, even though it is expressed in your own words, must be footnoted: if you say that by the time Nixon resigned, the American system of justice had suffered almost irreparable harm, you must tell readers the source of this opinion if it is not your own idea.

Quotations

Anything you quote from one of your sources must of course be footnoted in your paper. Sometimes it's tempting to crowd in quotations all over the place; other authors may have said just what you want to express, and they may have said it better than you think you can. Resist this temptation! A term paper that's just a collection of lengthy quotes strung together with a sentence or two in between is a poor one. It's difficult to read. It jumps from one writer's style to another's without ever achieving a style of its own. And this kind of hodgepodge leaves very little room for you to express your own ideas and thoughts.

Use quotes sparingly. A few well-chosen quotations from other writers will give support to your arguments without interfering with the flow of your thoughts. The function of quotations is to provide evidence for the key points you want to make. So don't throw in random quotes just to prove to your teacher that you've read the source material. Make them count!

When you've chosen a quotation, cut it down as much as you can. The reason you're repeating someone else's words is that the author has captured a concept in especially vivid or dramatic language. So save only the pithy phrase or succinct sentence that says exactly what you want; leave out the rest of the paragraph.

Whom should you quote? Both primary and secondary sources can provide quotable passages. Primary sources are any papers written at the time you are dealing with, or written by or to the people who were involved. These are "firsthand" or contemporary documents. Secondary sources are generally books written about the subject at a later date. They are "secondhand," written at one remove from the subject.

Depending on your topic, you may use more of one kind or the other. For example, if your paper is about the Emancipation Proclamation, you may find lots of primary sources: the Proclamation itself, any letters, diaries, or other papers of the time that concern the Proclamation, immediate newspaper reports about it, firsthand accounts of how the Proclamation was received by the public. But if your subject is the changing views of the Reconstruction Era, you'll use only secondary sources: histories of Reconstruction that have been written from the turn of the century up to the present.

If there is a great deal of primary source material available on your subject, you will probably quote quite a lot. A paper on some aspect of the Watergate cover-up will certainly include liberal splashes of testimony from the Senate investigation. The problem here will be to pick out the illuminating comments from the wealth of quotable material.

If you're quoting mostly from secondary sources, you should choose your quotes carefully, limiting both the number of quotes and their length. Pick quotes from authors who write especially well or who are recognized experts in the field.

What's Your Contribution?

A term paper is supposed to be an original piece of writing. But no one expects you to come up with a totally new theory of why the Civil War began! On the other hand, you can't just regurgitate the same information you found in your sources without adding anything of your own.

You may wonder how you can be original when everything you've learned on your topic comes from books written by other people. Won't you just be retelling their ideas in your own words?

Not if you've really given thought to what you want to say. For instance, if your subject is the causes of the Civil War, you may have read one book that says the causes were mainly economic, while another source emphasizes the social and moral causes. Reading these books should have led you to think about their ideas. You may decide that both authors are convincing to some extent, but that both of them overlooked the political factors. Saying this in your paper is your contribution; it is the result of your having absorbed what you've learned and come up with your own point of view on the subject. This is what makes your term paper original and keeps it from being merely a list of what some other people think.

Remember, you chose your topic in the first place because you thought it was interesting. You probably do have your own ideas about it and some things you want to say. Don't let yourself get bogged down with too much concern about quotes and sources. Just write down what you have to say on the subject and use quotes and footnoted facts to support and give examples for the points you're making. This way your own enthusiasm will come through in your writing and the final product will be genuinely original.

Follow the Form

Footnotes and bibliographies are supposed to be written in a standard form. After all, the reason for footnotes and bibliographies is to provide readers with the information they need to find your source material and read it themselves if they want to. Therefore, the standard form includes the author's name, the title of the work, the facts of publication (publisher, place, and date) and, in the case of footnotes, the page number where the quote or fact can be found.

Here is a sample of the form for footnotes and bibliographies recommended by *The MLA Style Sheet.*

Footnotes:

BOOK:

   [1]Elizabeth James and Carol Barkin, How to Keep a Secret: Writing and Talking in Code (New York: Lothrop, Lee & Shepard Co., 1978), p. 39.

MAGAZINE ARTICLE:

   [2]S.E. Crane, "Reading Chinese Tea Leaves," Commonweal, 104 (24 June 1977), 394.

ENCYCLOPEDIA ARTICLE:

   [3]"Civil War, American," Compton's Encyclopedia, 1969 ed., 5, 375.

Bibliography:

BOOK:

James, Elizabeth, and Carol Barkin. How to Keep

   a Secret: Writing and Talking in Code. New

   York: Lothrop, Lee & Shepard Co., 1978.

MAGAZINE ARTICLE:

Crane, S.E. "Reading Chinese Tea Leaves,"

   Commonweal, 104 (24 June 1977), 393-97.

ENCYCLOPEDIA ARTICLE:

"Civil War, American," Compton's Encyclopedia,

   1969 ed., 5, 372-79.

Notice that there are some obvious differences in form between footnotes and bibliography entries. In a footnote, the author's name is given in normal order; the first line is indented and the rest of the note is not; the punctuation used is commas and parentheses. In a bibliography entry, the name of the author (the first author only if there are more than one) is given in reverse order; this is because the books in a bibliography are listed in alphabetical order according to authors' last names. A book listing in a bibliography is punctuated with periods and no parentheses. The first line is started at the margin, with the rest of the entry indented.

Footnotes are usually numbered consecutively through the term paper. That is, you don't start over with footnote number 1 on each page. Type or write the numbers of the footnotes a little above the text. The footnotes themselves should be typed single-space at the bottom of each page.

What if you have more than one footnote referring to the same source? You need not use the full form for any but the first reference to each source. Instead, you can use two Latin abbreviations.

Ibid. is short for *ibidem,* which means "in the same place." If the source you refer to is the same as the source in the footnote immediately preceding, use *Ibid.* and the page number. If you are referring to a source you've already cited, but it's not the source in the footnote just above, you can use the abbreviation *op. cit.* This stands for *opere citato*, which means "in the work already cited." Give the author's last name, then *op. cit.*, and then the page number (Bakeless, *op. cit.*, p. 16.).

These abbreviations save space, and they prevent too many repetitions of the same information you've already provided. However, some teachers prefer that you use a shortened form of the author's name and the book's title for subsequent references to the same source, instead of the Latin terms. This method is actually clearer for your reader, and it's just as brief. You should follow your teacher's preference, since part of your grade may depend on how well you have followed instructions.

There are many minor variations on the standard forms given here. Be sure to find out *exactly* what form your teacher wants you to use in your term paper. If there is a book or mimeographed sheet giving this information, don't lose it! If you copy it down from the blackboard, be sure to copy everything accurately, down to the last period and comma. You may think these are just picky de-

cavalry men were able to move through the countryside more easily than unmounted soldiers. Also, cavalry officers were, usually men from wealthy families who felt superior to ordinary soldiers, and their fierce sense of loyalty to the Confederate cause made it an honor for them to do the dangerous work of spying.

The Confederates' civilian spy system was also superb. Many different kinds of people, from all walks of life, worked as spies under the Yankees' noses. In fact, "...a number of Southern women residing in the North continued to spy right through the war."[4] It is surprising to discover the vast extent of the spy system that passed invaluable information to the Confederate military and political leaders. In Washington, D.C. itself, for example, three different spy rings were in operation during the war. They were run by Mrs. Greenhow, Captain Conrad, and Frank String-fellow.[5]

Mrs. Greenhow's spy ring shows very clearly how easily the Confederates were able to penetrate the highest circles of Northern leadership. She was a well-known

[4]John Bakeless, Spies of the Confederacy, (Philadelphia: J.B. Lippincott Co., 1970), p. 65.
[5]Ibid., p. 6.

This sample page from a term paper shows a prescribed style for footnotes.

tails, and they are. But following the form exactly ensures that you don't leave out any of the information that must be included, and it keeps the reader from getting confused. And besides, even if your term paper is the best thing ever written, you won't get an A+ on it if your footnotes and bibliography are not done correctly!

Writing All Right?

No one can really define what makes good writing. But there are some things that can be said with certainty.

• Simple is better than needlessly complex. Don't be afraid of using short sentences and straightforward language.

• Say what you mean clearly. This may mean using short sentences and simple words. But primarily it means that you must think through what you are saying and then write it down in a way that the reader can follow. Garbled thoughts and tangled sentences make it look as though you don't have any idea of what you're doing.

• Don't use a long word where a short one will do. Many beginning writers mistakenly believe that fancy words give their writing more "class." And other writers seem to use a string of long words in the hope that readers won't notice that they really have nothing to say. Don't try to impress people with the number of syllables in your words; instead, dazzle them with the clear, understandable way you can express your ideas.

• Don't talk down to your reader; at the same time, don't assume that he or she knows as much as you do about your subject. Take time to explain things as fully as necessary. Other people can only read your paper—they can't read your mind!

Tools of the Trade

There are lots of books available that can help you with various aspects of writing. A dictionary, of course, is basic. And it isn't designed to help you only with your spelling, although it does a good job of that. It is also the place to find out whether a word you plan to use really means what you think it does. Any dictionary is better than none. But if you're buying one, it's worth the extra money to get a medium-sized hardbound volume, such as Webster's Collegiate. Paperbound dictionaries are hard to read; also, they don't stay open to the page you're looking at, and the pages start falling out after you've used them a few times.

A thesaurus is another useful tool for writers. It is a dictionary of synonyms; when you're looking for another way to say "interesting" or "nice," a thesaurus will help you out. You won't use it as often as you use a dictionary, so in this case a paperback might be a good idea; or look for a secondhand thesaurus, since they don't go out of date the way dictionaries do. If you don't own either a dictionary or a thesaurus, why not add them to your birthday or Christmas list?

If you have problems with grammar, ask your teacher to recommend a book that will help. There are many good ones, but it's probably smart to refer to one that's used in your school system.

Books about writing—style, composition, use of language—can be found in any school or public library. They offer advice about various problems that writers wrestle with. You may be surprised to find that many of these books, though filled with genuinely helpful information, are written in an ironic or humorous vein; they are really a pleasure to read, and you may find yourself browsing through their pages long after you've located the parts you were looking for.

Possibly the best book on writing is *The Elements of Style*, by William Strunk, Jr., and E. B. White. It's funny; it's short; and if you follow the advice it contains, you can't help becoming a better writer. It comes in paperback as well as hardcover; buy it and read it. Then tackle your term paper again with renewed energy and gusto.

7

How Do You Like It?

At last your first draft is finished. Now it's time for the final polish. As you turn back to page 1, you may have a sinking feeling that the whole thing is going to sound totally stupid and boring. This is a common reaction.

At the opposite extreme, you may start rereading and find you're completely in love with every word you wrote. It all sounds wonderful and you're amazed that you wrote such brilliant prose.

Neither of these ideas is likely to be true. What you've written is probably pretty good, but it's a rare author whose work doesn't need a little fixing up.

One way to avoid these reactions is to take a break and let your first draft sit for a while. Watch television (but don't get hooked and forget to go back to work!), read a paperback thriller, go out jogging—anything to take your mind off what you've written. If you have time to leave it overnight, that's great. But even half an hour away from it will bring you back to your term paper with a fresh eye.

What Did You Say?

The first rereading of your paper is for content. Does it say what you set out to say? Does it make sense? Does each thought follow logically from the one before? Have you left out anything? Or have you said the same thing twice?

You may find a section that sounds perfectly okay on its own but that doesn't seem to belong where it is. Don't bother to rewrite it. Just get out your scissors and tape and stick it where it does belong. It may need a couple of minor changes, but that's easier than rewriting the whole thing. "Cut and paste" is a time-honored method of revising all kinds of writing; don't be afraid to try it.

If you need to add a whole paragraph, perhaps an explanation you skipped over too fast, write it on a separate sheet of paper and then cut and paste it in. But if you're just adding a sentence to make a transition from one idea to the next, you can write it in the space between the lines. Make sure you'll be able to read it later, though!

What if your paper is too long? Now is the time to trim it down to size. Look for ideas that are presented more than once and take out the repetitions. Compare the length of the various sections:

if one is much longer than the others, this may be the part to concentrate on. You're likely to find too many quotes or examples here, or too elaborate explanations. If you do discover that you've made exactly the same point twice in different words, keep the one that's more vivid and forceful and cross out the other.

A paper that's too short is a different matter. First check the paper against your outline to make sure you've covered everything; you may have left out a whole section or skimped on explanations your reader will need. Maybe there are a couple of good quotes or some interesting information you didn't include the first time through; insert these at the appropriate places in the paper. But do keep in mind that "too short" is a relative term. If your paper is nine and a half instead of ten pages long, don't pad it with irrelevant or boring stuff just to make it a few lines longer. Few term papers come out to precisely the right length.

Even though you followed your outline, you may find that your finished draft doesn't exactly match the outline's construction. Perhaps, as you wrote, you realized that a section you planned to write near the beginning really belonged toward the end. Or you may have done some cutting and pasting because the sequence of ideas seemed to work better another way.

This is fine. Outlines are not meant to be followed slavishly down to the last subsection. If you've improved on your original structure for the paper, you've obviously kept your creative juices flowing all along. However, if your outline has to be turned in with the term paper, you may want to consider revising it to match the final product. Some teachers use the outline as a table of contents or a quick guide to what your paper says; an outline that doesn't show your paper's actual construction will just be confusing. On the other hand, if your teacher wants to see the steps you've gone through in the creative process, there's no need to revise your outline to match the final draft.

How Does It Sound?

Now that you're satisfied with the content and structure of your paper, you're ready to give it a critical reading to check on language, style, grammar, and spelling. A good way to begin is to read the paper aloud or to ask someone to read it while you listen. You'll pick up lots of little problems this way. Incomplete sentences, for instance, will bring the reader to an abrupt halt. You'll also be able to hear repetitious words and phrases, and you'll identify complicated passages that are impossible to follow.

Next, go through the paper one paragraph at a time with pencil in hand. Are all the sentences complete? Fix any that are not. Check your punctuation, and look up any words whose spelling you are unsure of. Look at the construction of your sentences. Do they all begin with "There were" or "He said" or "However"? Are they all the same length, and do they all follow the same pattern of subject-predicate-object? It's easy to fall into a boring pattern. Try turning a sentence into a question. Or have you thought of varying construction in other ways—maybe combining two sentences, or splitting a long one into two parts?

Certain words are often overused—not only adjectives and adverbs, but even nouns and verbs. Find synonyms for adjectives and adverbs, or get rid of them entirely in some places; often a strong verb will do the job better. However, sometimes it's hard to avoid repetition. If your paper is about Abraham Lincoln, you may find yourself using "the President," "Lincoln," and "he" over and over. Vary it as much as you can. Try writing

"Mr. Lincoln" now and then, or even "Abe" if it's appropriate, and turn some of your sentences around so they don't all begin with Lincoln's name. But don't go overboard with far-out alternatives; it's best to avoid phrases like "the rail-splitter" or "the self-taught bearded giant."

Don't forget to look at each paragraph as a whole. Does it hang together logically? You may find that one long paragraph needs to be broken into two, or that two short ones would work better if you combined them into one. Don't feel you must make them all the same length, however; it's more interesting to read a paper that has some variety. Make sure you aren't starting every paragraph with identical phrasing or words; if they all begin with "On the other hand" or "If," you'll need to change some.

Neatness Counts

Now that your paper says what you want to say the way you want to say it, you're ready to make your final copy. You may think neatness is only for little old ladies, but look at it this way: a neatly presented paper has a built-in advantage.

How would you like to plow through thirty papers, puzzling out the sloppy handwriting before you could even figure out what they were trying to say?

If at all possible, type your term paper. Or at least write slowly and carefully so it will be easy to read. A typed paper should be double-spaced; if yours is to be hand-written, ask your teacher what to do about spacing. In any event, use blue or black ink. Wild colors like purple or green only distract the reader, so save them for Christmas cards. And of course never write a final draft in pencil, which is too easy to smudge or erase.

Write or type on one side of the paper only, and leave generous margins all around. The written material should be "framed" by white space, not only at the top and sides but also at the bottom. Wide margins make your text easier and more pleasant to read; you've probably noticed this yourself in books and magazines.

Pay attention when your teacher hands out the form sheet you are to follow or explains the way your paper should be set up. If page numbers are to be in the upper right-hand corner, put them there. Stop writing or typing soon enough to leave space for footnotes; they shouldn't fall off the bottom of the page. Make sure your name is on each page, in case a whole stack of term papers is dropped on the floor.

When your final draft is finished, check it over for spelling mistakes. If spelling is your worst subject, ask a friend with an eagle eye to check it for you. This is a good idea in any case; it's harder to spot your own errors than to see someone else's. You can correct spelling errors neatly in ink, but it's probably best to retype or rewrite a page that has a lot of corrections.

Now you're all set and it's only two o'clock in the morning! Gather up your pages together with your bibliography and get out the stapler. But wait! What about your title page?

This is your last chance to make sure the title you started out with is still appropriate. Do you still like it? Can you think of anything better?

Many people think titles are harder to write than the paper itself. A title should tell your reader what your paper is about. Straightforward titles are fine, but keep them short; your entire summary sentence probably won't make a good title.

Everyone wants a title that grabs a reader's attention immediately, but be a little cautious about this. Don't get so carried away with clever wording that your meaning gets lost. And be fairly specific—if your paper is about the battle of Gettysburg, don't entitle it "The Civil War."

Goodbye and Good Luck!

Now that it's all over, it really wasn't so bad, was it? No one gets through school without writing a term paper, and almost everyone survives the experience! And when you think about it, writing a term paper has a lot to be said for it —it's more creative than conjugating verbs or memorizing theorems. In fact, it's one of the few chances you get in school to decide what you want to do and how you want to do it. And who knows? You may even find that it's fun to delve into a subject you're interested in and that you really enjoy expressing your ideas in writing.

Bibliography

Corder, Jim W. *Handbook of Current English.* 5th ed. Glenview, Ill.: Scott, Foresman, & Co., 1978.

    A very complete and clearly presented guide to all aspects of English composition, with excellent sections on preparing and writing term papers.

Manual of Style. 12th ed., revised. Chicago: University of Chicago Press, 1969.

    Contains the answer to every question you may have about writing formal papers; follows the style preferred by the University of Chicago Press and many other publishers.

MLA Style Sheet. Revised ed. Compiled by William Riley Parker. New York: Modern Language Association of America, 1951.

    A brief guide to the style preferred by the Modern Language Association; along with the Chicago *Manual*, an acknowledged authority in questions of formal writing.

Strunk, William, Jr., and E. B. White. *The Elements of Style.* 3rd ed. New York: The Macmillan Co., 1979.

    In our opinion, the best guide to good writing for students or anyone else. Brief, funny, memorable, and always to the point.

Turabian, Kate L. *Student's Guide for Writing College Papers.* 3rd ed. Chicago: University of Chicago Press, 1976.

    A helpful tool for finding one's way through the complexities of preparing a paper; useful for high school as well as college work.

Index

Elizabeth James and Carol Barkin have tried both ways of writing term papers: wait-till-the-last-minute and following the principles outlined in this book. Fortunately, they are as well organized separately as they are together, for although they live at opposite ends of the continent, they have collaborated successfully on more than a dozen books.

Elizabeth James received her B.A. in mathematics from Colorado College, where she minored in experimental psychology. She and her husband live in Beverly Hills, California.

Carol Barkin received her B.A. from Radcliffe College, where she majored in English. Formerly a children's book editor, Ms. Barkin is now a full-time writer. She and her husband live in Hastings-on-Hudson, New York, with their young son.